SAWTOOTH **WAVES**

Charleston, SC
www.PalmettoPublishing.com

Sawtooth Waves
Copyright © 2023 by Ben Schulz

First Edition

Paperback ISBN: 979-8-8229-1211-3

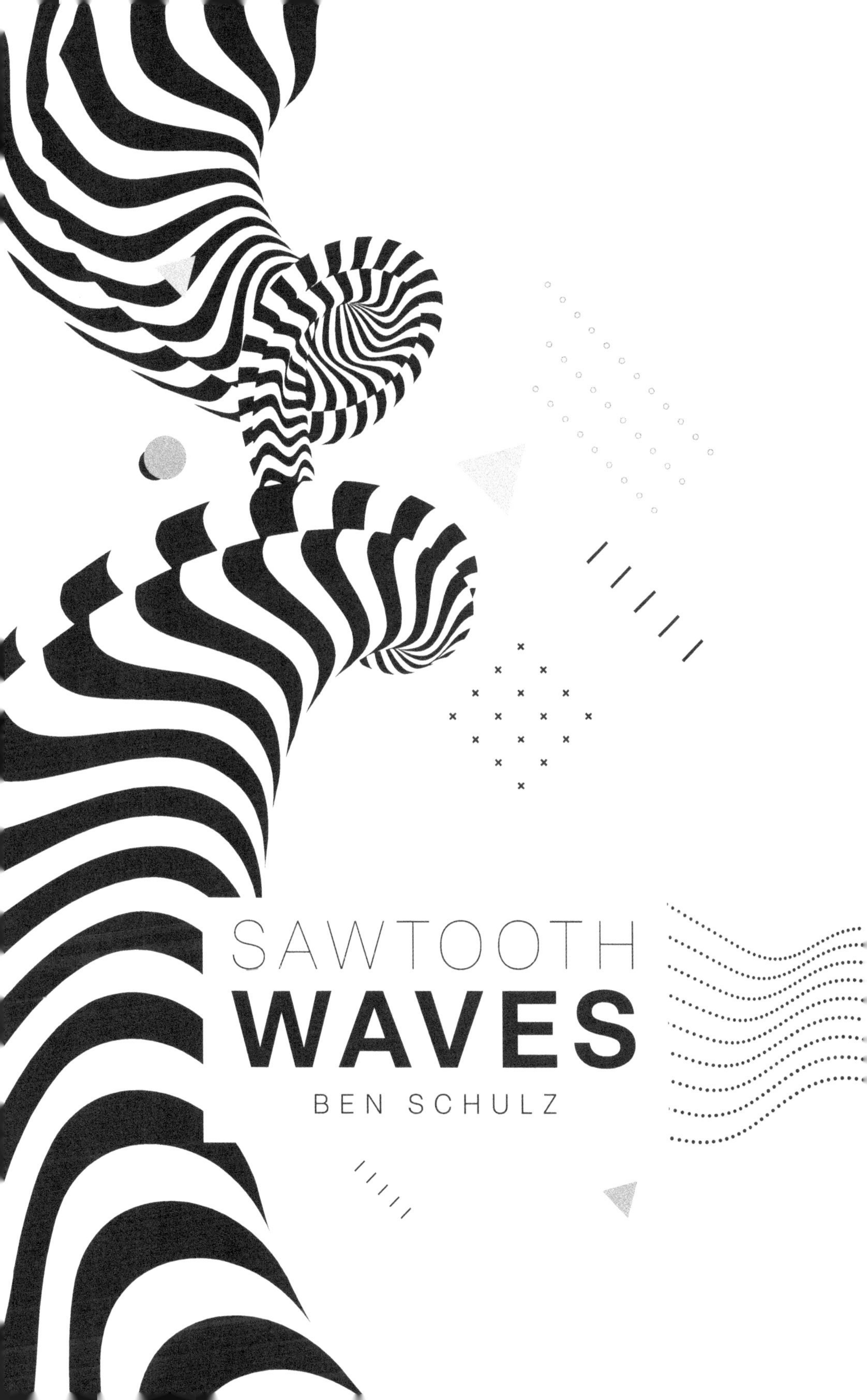

SAWTOOTH
WAVES
BEN SCHULZ

25 POEMS

S A W T O O T H   W A V E S

He rises and falls like a sawtooth waveform.
Tough times cannot clamp onto him.
Threatened by a backyard rebellion,
He smiles with sawtooth teeth.
He points northward and always stays on his post.
His songs are like feathers,
Stuffed inside an excavator bucket,
Held together by an arch clip.
You say, "He is swimming in a moribund genre?"
Bosh, I say. He makes waves.
Sawtooth Waves.
He breaks on the shore and
Coils back to the sea.

FIBERS OF SISAL

When looking for good rope,
Versatile and durable,
I recommend the sisal.
Fibers of sisal are stiff—
Sentinels of the agave plant.
Their swordlike leaves,
5 feet long,
Protect the town of Sisal
on the Yucatan Peninsula.
Soaking
every day under the fiery sun,
refusing to stand down.
Prospective invaders thwarted.
Generations ago, the trabajadores
crushed the leaves,
to squeeze
out soft plant juices.
Decorticating, it's called.
the coarse remains are scraped,
washed, and dried.

Does sisal rope hang in your shed?
They hold knots like barbed wire;
they can wrap a gift, fasten hay bales,
tie off canvas sails,
and squeeze tight the arboles
de Navidad.
The Fibers of sisal refuse to wilt,
And can hold your life
Together.

HENRY STONE

Henry Stone was a widow.
Alone in a thatched cottage, he rotated
His vinegar bottles on the table,
Using his swollen fingers.
Slow rain. Bone needles on wall.
Navigation in his soul.
Had a cat named Tiger.
Hours of silence interrupted with
New meows,
Like a branch that rubs across the
Window.
Stone was New blood in 1717,
Emerged from the European waves.
New World dreams,
Beaufort Precinct, North Carolina.

Memories strong as
Silver coins. Yellow Neck kerchief.
Laughter bounces off the river.
But new dreams begat new tragedy—
Occasional fogs, blue moods,
His wife was taken too soon.
Emptiness on the
Once-bustling Pamlico River.
Buried her leather shoes
Beneath pine floorboards
And it would bring good luck
To his property
Which he called Lynbrook.

They stuffed his shells with little balls.
He promised them Acid Fire. Steel Rain.
They say he helped beat Napoleon at Waterloo
with his genius, and deadly skills, and devastating talent.
Shrapnel studied the trajectories and timing,
the arc through space, over open fields of clover.
The big guns thundered, the commanders
watched the "bombs bursting in air."
Like a popped bubble, a fragmentary burst.
An evening sky could light up with its
burning and piercing and high-lighted mass.
The horses jumped; men hit the deck.
The explosions Shrapnel wrought
would illuminate the oak wood,
the tall crops of rye, the old kitchen gardens,
the crossroads, the baggage wagons,
an innocent-looking landscape;
ancient warfare shuddered. Shrapnel
brought the "shrapnel" that left the enemy
injured, maimed, and killed, like
a nightmare.

THE QUAKING BOG

The peat accumulates under the mat—
swallowed in acidity and low oxygen,
—and shows
bursting decay of time.
A heavy fog reveals
grey vines and flimsy shoots.
Ferns and sedges explode with
triangular smiles.
The sundews and pitcher plants thrive
in the poor drainage.
Atop red and brown carpets, the
slick frogs and beetles chirp and click.

Larger trees are absent in the quaking bog;
their roots cannot take hold
along the slimy sedges.
(For, a woodsman
cannot construct a hardy fence made
of wet paper.)
The floating mat,
cool and wet, rolls on and on
like a rug of sponges.
The dragonflies police the area known as
the quaking bog, as
a cold wind blows off the Bay.

THE GREAT LEAP

The bourgeois should shine,
most European leaders
told us.
Whoever steered production
will define a brand-new century.
But in Russia,
there was a Great Leap,
a great offensive,
a bald irony—
Stalin destroyed class struggle:
we pushed men down like rats
and leveled the field.
Although this "command economy"
produced industrial plants,
petroleum repositories,
the Trans-Siberian Railway,
and fielded great fighting armies,
the situation was perverse.
Nobody shined. The rats woke up dead.
Russia was incapable of real advancement.
The absence of a middle class,
or bourgeois, was the real killer.
Not Western capitalism.
It was a Great Leap—
And terrific fall.

I'm a Tom.
I'm a Dick.
I'm a Harry.
Not just any Tom, Dick, or Harry.

My favorite color fills arenas and makes waves.
I study unprompted mannerisms.
I take long steps, but small strides.
I smile when I think about firewood, and
Corn Dog Festivals.

I enjoy apples and oranges, but I hate when
my dog says, "That's like apples and oranges."
I enjoy legal stimulants, like turnips.
My bumper sticker—*Treasure the Turnip*—
is a prized possession.
My dog coaches me to zero in, penetrate
the pins on the ball track,
"frightful collisions may happen,
but the key is in the grip."
It's not about the target—the pins,
the catcher's mitt, the bullseye;
it's about leverage and weight and energy
And ice-cold mechanics.
And mental toughness.

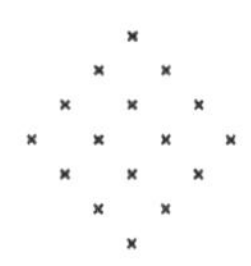

A Koufax breaking ball in 1965
comes in belt high but falls,
gloriously, to your knee
And you swing over it.
Happiness is a sturdy bridge.
Pierre Bonnard's brush and Albert Camus's voice.
Happiness is successfully returning
your shopping cart into the
parking lot receptacle,
back to his family and not alone,
staring at some Subaru's ass.
That's who I am, dammit.
I see myself as a Tom;
others have called me a Dick.
I'm not just any Tom, Dick, or Harry!
That's like apples and oranges.

MY BIRD DID NOT DROP

On Monday I met a sparrow hawk; his name was Batty Langley.

37 centimeters. With strips of kangaroo leather,

I created jesses for his legs.

On Tuesday me and Batty watched Battleship Potemkin and had popcorn.

He asked for a bike for Christmas.

On Wednesday I altered his jesses and took wide loops in the sky and

Dives inside my head. He told me, "Sir Walter Raleigh was fond of hawking."

On Thursday we ate chickens. I taught Batty how to read.

That is, to read certain situations...

On Friday I removed his jesses and then I drank from the river. I threw out the trash and

Threw out my back.

On Saturday Batty Langley flew away, forever.

My bird did not drop. I was alone

With the Scioto trees and other people's birds.

Behold, ye angels and assassins! My bird did not drop.

Protect him.

On Sunday I looked at the old jesse set and reminded myself that I was

A falconer. I was an honorable fellow.

I helped Batty spread his wings,

See the green earth, in search of

The brightest suns,

And I smiled inside the mist.

Holding the unattached jesses,

I could still smell Batty's feathers and feet.

Behold! The skies are quiet. My bird did not drop.

Life in the 79th Ohio was more exciting.
I'm out here now, collecting arrowheads,
Strumming my banjo, letting my beard grow.
I tried rattlesnake yesterday, with habanero sauce.

I escaped harm at Antietam, now wounded
by boredom. My King James, warped and beaten,
keeps me company. At night I study the stars;
they are my wife and daughter, so brilliant but so far off.

I exhale off my pipe and wait through the night
for the post to come. So dark and barren.
I hear they got lamps in New Jersey that light up at night!

Lord, grant me a furlough to see my daughter.
I want to read a newspaper, sip champagne,
go to a tailor, take my family to a show.
America had her 100th birthday and I'm out here.

INSTALLATION ARTIST

She filled a bowler hat with sticky honey.
She built a men's suit using toothpicks.
She drops water
Across the room and out of frame —
The echo upon impact is undulating and Heavy.
It's so loud, you can see it.
Her visuals are so overwhelming,
You can hear it.
Bees, canaries, and flesh-eating beetles abound
in a kaleidoscope of color.
Her viewers experience a sudden chill
when
cool water drips
down a "human" neck, and
they listen, helplessly, to haunting chants,
and they watch, uncomfortably, a mime artist moving
robotically in repetitive gesture,
a face plastered with joy.
She dazzles in installation art.
After the show, you are told that the mime
Was the artist herself.

WHITE RUSSIA

There's permafrost beneath my tank. White Russia.
Cold mud puddles, and dank.
Pass me on the street,
Pass me, marching feet,
Pass me, you're beat. White Russia.

April evacuation.
Burn down Richmond station.
Global manifestation.
Pass me on the street,
Pass me, marching feet,
Pass me, you're beat.
Napoleon's retreat. White Russia.

Russian ice cubes melt.
Our valued cards are dealt.
Another notch, heather gray belt.
I remember. White Russia.
I remember. White Russia.

Your retreat sudden, moving fast!
Your ice cubes a thing of the past.
War's outcome has been cast
Pass me on the street, White.
Pass me, marching feet, Russia.
Pass me, you're beat.
White Russia.

Pre-dawn blackness begins to lift at 6 am.
Cirrus clouds—they seem to blanket the cold
universe—want to turn pink;
their cousins Stratus are like dark submarines on patrol.
They glide softly to the south, ensuring
that the sun stays out of sight and that the sky
remains mysterious.
Things swim overhead, adrift at sea, shapes of
disconnected jigsaw puzzle pieces and
more submarines and clusters of gray seaweed.
Pink fades to light gray, light gray fades
to white with touches of grayish blue.
Still the sun is backstage. The Southern Rockies
are outlined majestically against the gray sky at 6:40.
32 degrees. The horizon to the east is crystal-like,
whispering to northern New Mexico
promises of snow. The sun is holding out, on strike.
The stratus submarines motor away.
The snow clouds will soon report to work, as their
predecessors go home, like a change
of administrations.
We wait—me and dozens of pinon trees.
I weave in and out of my friends; they're in no
hurry. We're all journeymen waiting at a train station,
checking our watches, ready to
discuss the weather.

Pliny the Elder
Could tell you when the chickweed grows
Or why Roman martens scuttle.
He was a master in
Etiquette and minerals,
Rhetoric and philosophy,
Medicine and birds.

Pliny the Elder told me,
My subject is a barren one—
The world of nature, or in other words Life.

Life is a serpent, though the snake was bitten.
Memories under layers of lava flows.
The earth swallowed the mastermind,
Pliny the Elder,
Who could tell you when the chickweed grows.

Pliny the Elder told me,
My subject is a barren one—
The world of nature, or in other words Life.
He was a master in
Etiquette and minerals,
Rhetoric and philosophy,
Medicine and birds.

DRY SOUND

Cove inlets take me, somewhere.
Moon pointing, rising fresh air.
Combing waters, I see her breath there
over the dry sound.

Road winding, fore and aft.
Swallow your stares. Stairway's cast.
Like you more, more than *that*
over the dry sound.
Again and again, we skirt the waters, we hover
over the dry sound.
Again and again, we skirt the waters and we trouble
and then you sigh.
Again! Over the dry sound.
Again! Over the dry sound.
Not afraid of unseen melody.
Grounded, nothing breaks me.
Courage: nothing can take me.
Blindfold swept, she slept beside me—
over the dry sound.
Again! Over the dry—and then you sigh—
Dry sound.
The moon on the road,
soon it explodes,
over the dry sound.

THE 1968 RECORD

(on which Lovely Rita gives up her seat to Desmond and Molly)
The Summer of Love—
bright sentimental sunshine—was so last year.
Retrospect? Too much gloss, squeaky-cleanness, with
dreamy strings that
ECHO.
Echo
echo. Many said, Perfection achieved.
Swinging London, guys with mustaches
and Pinstripe pants.

The new 1968 record will be different,
giant and clumsy; each track a rough-hewn freshness,
like when you split apart dry hickory. The scraps and
splinters will dangle, carefree
and random.

How many songs, 12? NO
30! Little gemstones,
rattling inside a washing machine. Different
colors, shapes, origins. Hear the clanging after
you slam the square door and press the button.
Martha, you are captured, my dear.
The common theme is, there is no common theme.
"No-one will be watching us!" he screams, slamming his piano.
Stripped down, raw, heavy.
Not easy listening. Doesn't even
have to be radio-friendly, honey pie.

Last year, "happiness" was Lucy with her Diamonds; this year it's
a Warm Gun.

Because it's not about power or trends,
or upward momentum,
or money or sex or more drugs.
It's about...Me and my monkey; blackbirds; hobnail boots;
weeping guitars; country-western meets heavy metal, meets soft
acoustic meets open-mike poetry.
"Cool cherry cream, nice apple tart."
Last year, I was fixing a hole where the rain gets in,
This year, I've got blisters on my fingers.

The critics won't get it, won't even know where to
begin, their pencils and pads at the ready.
Listening to—sorting through?—the mishmash.
"Gee it's good to be back home." "However big you think you are."
You will listen to each song 4 or 5 times,
to simply digest.
Disorganized clutter rules the day; the girl
stuffs rubber duckies and lollipops and Legos into a sturdy
doll house. It will be—not correct, but beautiful.
Ho-hum packaging, no ostentation. Stark.
Unmistakable.
It's a mark of a brilliant album when you
return the vinyl to its sleeve and say, WAIT—
these the same guys?
The lads on the lunch box?
Okay—
So what's the title? Doesn't have one.
Dear Prudence: you gotta hear this.

CONCRETE SOD

They embedded seashells in wet cement at a new city.
Then it dried and the people forgot about it
And the city matured, developed wrinkles.
Does anyone see Chance?
Does anyone see Irony?

The shells were frozen cold on the chalky sidewalks
In God's plan. They are entombed within
Eternal chance and convenience.
Lonely fabrics melt away.
The gate's locked.
Modest contributions sealed.
Now we rest in the concrete sod.

The search is spent.
Dead topics are stepped over.
Blind chance rules the universe.
The concrete sod is the pathway.
After 500 years in the
Concrete sod—I see it now—
I see Chance; I see Irony.
It was there the whole time,
In the concrete sod.

VULCANIZE THE CHICLE

Mexicans for generations have chewed "chicle."
Across dusty borders, many moons, and weekdays,
Tropical trees—sapodillas—yield milky latex.
Chicle will go far. A rubber substitute, thought best.
Vulcanize the chicle.

We can use it as rubber! Our carriages to have tires.
Our docks padding, our pipes protected from fires.
General Santa Anna brought some here in 1866.
He told Americans: "The gum and your future will mix."
He said, "Vulcanize the chicle."

A man named Adams thought, A rubber alternative, bosh!
Adams saw chewing gum, at a manageable cost.
The Mexicans must have chewed on this irony, frankly.
The Mexicans must not have found Adams to "thank ye."
Santa Anna, thinking rubber, died dead broke.
Adams became the richest business-minded bloke.

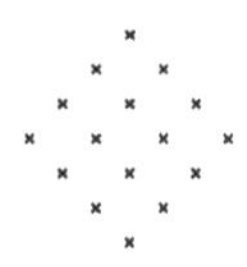

Vulcanize the chicle? Negative response.
Just add flavor and suck it, as is our wont.
Pleasing millions, dissatisfying only few
As poor Santa Anna bit off more than he could chew.
(He had said, "Vulcanize the chicle.")

Milky latex is pumped; we suck all day,
chew, grind and smile, only half dollar we pay.
Chicle, chicle, chicle—you are not vulcanized.
Chicle, you are sugared, flavored, caramelized.
Adams, thank you, and Santa Anna, gracias.
As milky latex is still pumped from sapodillas,
Vulcanize the chicle!

The darkness begins to lift;
cool pinks and yellows encroach along Q Street.
A city's bones and nerves and veins turned on by the sun—
the ghetto seafood carryout, slick with grease,
next to brick apartments, dripping condensation,
and the yoga joint, and
hundreds of city birds looking for scraps
next to Capital Bike Share,
under posters of Muriel Bowser
and Pride flags, bounding around the
bent Newport stubs.
The squirrels at the Baptist church,
beyond Safety cones and chain-link dividers
and one-way streets, frolicking.
The trash men hustle!
A construction man his Red Bull sipping,
the dog walkers yawning,
African cabbies and bike cops brush across the canvas:
big murals, big cracks in the street, big liquor stores with
big steel locks,
big rocks, a big sunrise.
We in Shaw blink at the sun.
We in Shaw circle back to Another promise.

L O O K   A T   T H E   C A N V A S

Stretched and turned in its queer abstraction. You
melt into the magnetic interference between
the teacup and the common fig,
atop a Dutch cutting board.
Estimate the proportions of the platter,
ripe cherries, shadows.
Dazzling in its centrifugal tendencies.
Everything held in place like a see-through paperclip.
Look at this one next,
neatly assorted inside hard angles.
Bacchus and Ariadne, naked with tigers
under exquisite constellations.
Look at the canvas.
You feel hot but the
landscape on the wall is frozen,
cemented,
behind your eyes,
processing the rectangular world.

YESTERDAY'S CHARMS

My thoughts today are of
Volcano girls,
Who relax by the sea,
The green wet sea,
Shapeless and soft and inviting,
Filled with yesterday's charms.
The villagers climb up the
Arch of Ancona and
Gaze out—
"Have you seen the Volcano girls?"
Your thoughts are swimming
On the watery planet and
Goodness and grace surround you.
Specimen exotic, saviors—
Muscle cells deplete; they will replace them.
Skin cells turned over; they will protect them.
Endothelial lining of your blood vessels; they will regenerate them.
We love your face.
We love your moisture.
We love yesterday's charms.
Today, however, it's not the same.
I discovered
It's a long way to see the
Volcano girls.

GUS HENDERSON

During spring,
Gus Henderson steps away from the
thinness of his day
and rises up
to a new search.
No more insurance sales and vapor gas.
No more soggy napkins.
Gus Henderson fought in Korea,
and he knew what he wanted:
clean dirt, smiling talent,
long hair, a roaring crowd,
good execution, a gallery of relevance,
wind and rain, a tasteful joke,
social studies, metaphor and morals,
cooperation and protection,
honesty and strategy.
Gus Henderson with white hair
Velcro-ed his shiny shoes,
drank his black cherry soda.
(break)
But then
Gus was knocked over
by the big government.
Fear merchants, death and suffering, prognosticate,
fear tactics, security, color, idiots, deception,
fear monger, curfews!

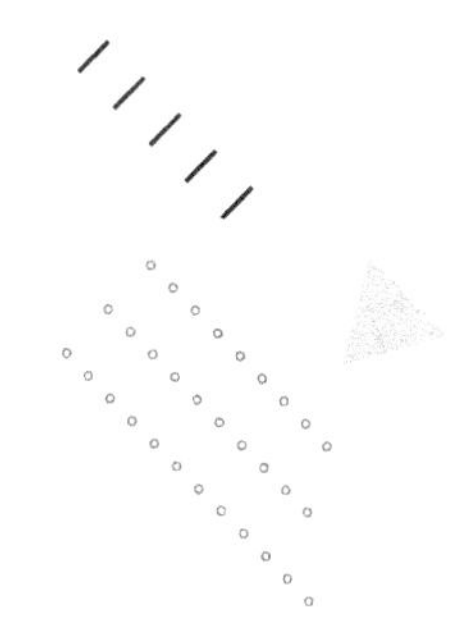

Data, worry, masks,
Grim milestone, criminal justice, doctors, experts,
scared and locked down, killer, risk, crisis,
high ratings, click bait, locked down, medical,
virus, riots, police, mayor, news, policy,
riots, virus, experts, news, illusions, ideas,
face coverings, under the thumb, social justice.
Wash your face and don't touch your hands.
Horse tranquilizer, puffy faces.
Scare them. You incite people.
Statistics, poverty, risks and curves, power,
overreach, agenda, buy in, China?
Briefings, mental health, respiratory therapists,
Looting, we are misled. Timing of life. Death.
Compliance, enforcement, science, streets,
race, Blacks, grim milestone, nursing homes,
scare them, no rationale, society, quarantine.

What is the truth? Shut them down. Closed.
Control the public.
Control the public.
Control the public.

Gus died in 2020.

Morning mist, a rising sun emits a glow,
The forests begin to chirp and hum.
The holly trees along Hunting Creek wave back and forth,
Green arms interlocked.
We make Ginseng tea and look at the boxwood fence,
Standing on our new oil cloth, marked artistically with
Large blue diamonds.
After breakfast Uncle lights up his clay pipe and tells us
To grab the linen sacks because we are heading down to
The wharf, past the village.
We walk down Banks Road, past the
slanting willows and a stack of fresh-hewn planks, towards
the sound of laughing children and a screaming rooster.
The man from the racing track is on the road, with
His chestnut mares, another man is selling his hog
next to his sandstone wall. Noon.
The river stretches her long body and is ready to dance.
The hucksters and merchants frolic like hens; they
Try to find shade alongside the huge warehouse next to
the stinky catfish, under the sign for "Hutton & Reed"
and they stand and talk with Uncle next to leather pails.
The Potomac, smiling, was stunning majesty. One of the boats
Brought thousands of oysters, and small iron pots; other
Boats brought in coffee and apples and figs. Uncle signs
The papers and we're ready to walk back,
Past the Negro sheds, with our heavy sacks full of
Snakeroot herb and hoecake mix. The sun was clear across

The sky and we saw oxen in the field; I was getting tired.
By the time we arrived home, I had forgotten about
The dust in my eyes, the stink of fish in my jacket, and the
Chorus of chatter and shouts at the warehouses at
Hutton & Reed.
That night we had pork, and Apple pie, and
William played his fiddle and
Uncle told us stories about the Potomac River.
After midnight, she was a watery bullwhip, cracked
Forward; all the little boats pushed to the mouth of
The Bay looking for new treasures.

LOCALIZED AND UNSEEN

Rip currents, powerful and dangerous,
can upend and throw you like when you
yank a cord and watch the corner lamp fly from its
perch, and smack
on the tiles.
You can't defeat the rip currents but you
may outsmart them.
They are localized and
unseen.
Concentrate; don't exhaust
yourself. Think.
Swim parallel to the shore until you break out of it;
they tend to be narrow. flank it.
Don't face the swarm of
bees head-on, but dart to one side with agility.
They will happily pass by.
Even though You are thinking of them,
they are not thinking of you.

There is a landing spot
For the free birds of
The Bay.
It is safe, away from
The lightning.
This way!
It is secure for
"All of 'em," I say.
There is a landing spot
For the free birds of
The Bay.
Up above the viruses
And the shouting
And cement troughs
And paparazzi. Here—okay?
There is a landing spot
For the free birds of
The Bay.

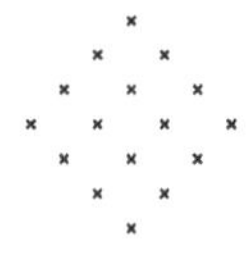

O, yeah. O, yeah. O, yeah.
Rest your head on a
pillow of severed branches.
Inside a shifting
Landscape, taking no chances.
Free Birds of
The Bay.
Solid footing, on the prowl.
Okay?
This way!
To the Bay. Today.
They always find a landing spot,
Above us, who use telephoto lenses
to survey private property or pursue targets in cars,
decidedly not free.

THE COLORS OF THE LOWER SHANNON

Stained and stroked, this land, by the handsome brush of antiquity.
The clouds don't move in, nor push out.
They gather and sit o'er the luxuriant country like
vultures on a medieval wall.
Gray is the sky; gray is the limestone plateaus,
and gray is the gothic friary.
Open the cherry-colored door and step inside the
stone dwelling, the color of concrete. And you
enter an Old World, beyond the Celtic Sea
and beyond recent annals.
White are the sheep dotting the Nire Valley.
Black is the mysterious insides of the O'Sullivan cottage,
black are the birds that swoop along River Furgus and
Along the timeworn tracks of Beckett and Shaw and Yeats.
Window shutters green; green are the pastures and moss clinging
to the cathedrals' arms and legs. And green
is the heartbeat and the soul; green is the nation, its pulse.
A decision is made by the sky—a soft rain falls on
Galway, Limerick, and Cork.
But the man with the brown pint flashes his yellow-stained teeth,
tells you the sun's a-coming to the Lower Shannon

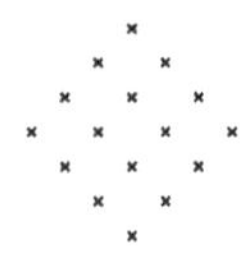

and you—you—
were in knee socks, wool vest, playing road bowling
in the clouds
at the valley of the Shannon.
We haven't met.
You are my best friend.

A F T E R W O R D

It starts out like an advertisement in an old magazine. Then it turns
into a sales pitch. She is self-effacing, allowing the story to appear
to tell itself. We compare our notes on the old measurements,
cubits, furlongs, frequency, and wavelength, and execute a
comprehensive analysis to ensure these can translate to the modern
age. Together, we check all mandatory boxes and then locate
a motivated buyer. She speaks with spirited wisdom. We avoid
sequence issues and as a result the trains run on time. The buyer is
dazzled. We sign the papers and pop the cork. But we cannot stay
complacent, she says, we must bend it back to somewhere unknown.
I agree and make sure to keep everything on a memory stick. Now
we can fall alien and impervious to the whirlwind of events.

—–-

I would like to thank Vanessa Dremé and Kelly Esparza for reading my
manuscript and offering valuable feedback.

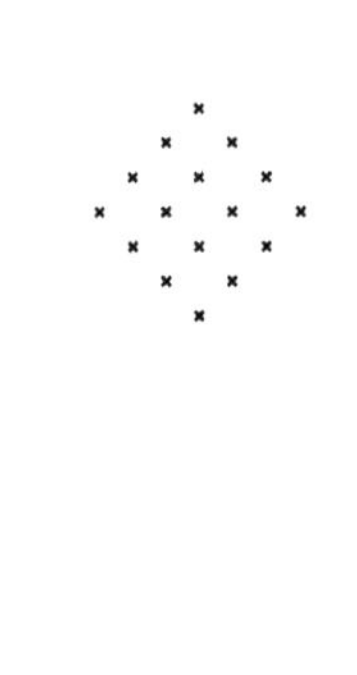